ASPECTS OF ROMAN LIFE

ROMAN SPORT AND ENTERTAINMENT

DAVID BUCHANAN
Douglas Ewart High School, Newton Stewart

LONGMAN

CONTENTS

1: Then and now Pages 1–4
Questions and Things To Do

2: Chariot races Pages 5–18
The Circus Maximus; Horses; Charioteers;
Diocles; A Day at the Races; Ben Hur;
A different view
Questions and Things To Do

3: Amphitheatres Pages 19–25
The Colosseum
Questions and Things To Do

4: Gladiators Pages 26–40
Two shows; Spartacus; Types of gladiators
and their equipment; The salute; A question
of thumbs; The Wooden Sword; Champions
and heart-throbs; Riot at Pompeii; The
taste of blood; The story of Alypius
Questions and Things To Do

5: Animal hunts and sea fights Pages 41–48
Performing animals; Beast fighters;
The slaughter of animals; Sea fights
Questions and Things To Do

6: Theatres Pages 49–61
Theatre of Orange; Theatre of St Albans;
Theatre of Marcellus; The stage;
The audience; Nero on the stage; Plays;
'The Menaechmus Brothers'; 'The Ghost'
Questions and Things To Do
Some important dates Page 62

1 : THEN AND NOW

What do you do for entertainment? Perhaps you watch a big sporting event, like the thousands at Wembley on Cup Final day. Or, perhaps you go to the cinema or theatre for a show. Or, again, perhaps, like millions all over the country, you stay at home and watch television.

We have a great deal of spare time and holidays in which to enjoy these things, and so did the ancient Romans. In the third century AD they had nearly two hundred public holidays in the year!

Aerial view of Wembley Stadium on Cup Final day

The Romans had no TV, of course, or cinemas, but they did have public shows, to which thousands went. The four main types of shows were chariot races, gladiator fights, animal hunts and plays.

a Circus Maximus **b** Colosseum **c** Theatre of Marcellus

The picture below shows a model of Rome in the fourth century AD, showing the buildings where these shows mainly took place: the **Circus Maximus** (chariot races), the **Colosseum** (gladiator fights and animal hunts), and the **Theatre of Marcellus** (plays).

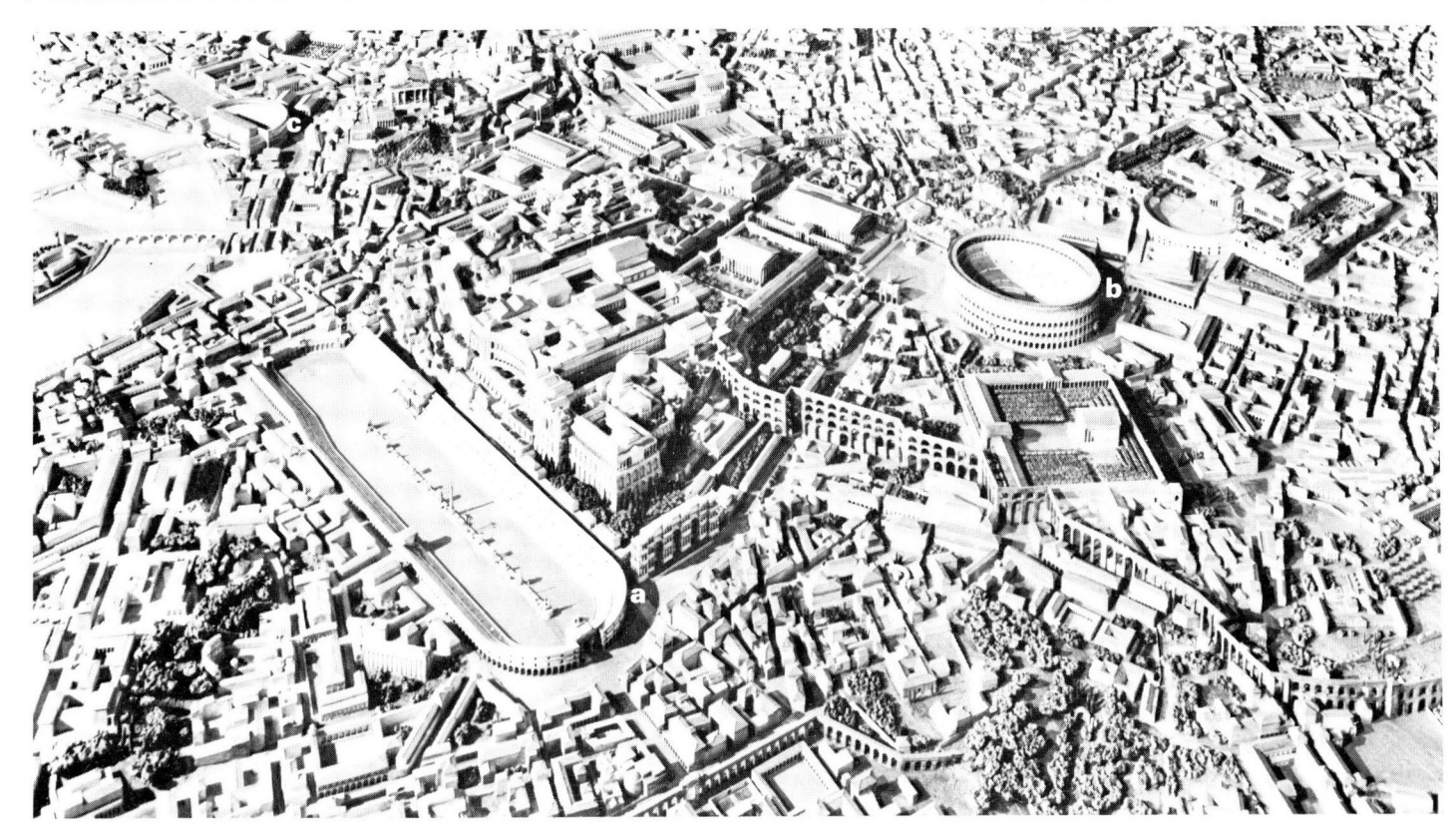

These entertainments were very popular with all classes of people in Rome, including the Emperors. Augustus, for example, used to watch the shows from the upper rooms of houses overlooking the Circus; he often said that he enjoyed the fun.

Nero was a 'fan' of the chariot races and came to Rome whenever they were on. He often drove chariots himself on his own track.

Claudius preferred gladiators and animal hunts. Sometimes he would send the audience away and watch the whole show in private.

Coin portraits of Augustus, Nero and Claudius

Augustus

Claudius

Nero

QUESTIONS

1. How many public holidays did the Romans have in the third century AD? What percentage (of 365) is this? (page 1)
2. What were the four main types of Roman shows and where were they held? (page 2)
3. Name the three Emperors who were 'fans' of the various shows. Say which shows each of them liked best. (page 3)

Holidays 1975

BRITISH
Jan. 1 New Year's Day
Mar. 28 Good Friday
Mar. 31 Easter Monday
May 18 Whitsun
May 26 Spring Bank Holiday
Aug. 25 Summer Bank Holiday
Dec. 25 Christmas Day
Dec. 26 Boxing Day

FRENCH
Jan. 1 New Year's Day
Mar. 31 Easter Monday
May 1 Labour Day
May 8 Ascension Day
May 19 Whit Monday
Jul. 14 National Day
Aug. 15 Assumption Day
Nov. 1 All Saint's Day
Nov. 11 Armistice Day
Dec. 25 Christmas Day

FEDERAL REPUBLIC OF GERMANY
Jan. 1 New Year's Day
Jan. 6 Epiphany
Mar. 28 Good Friday
Mar. 31 Easter Monday
May 1 Labour Day
May 8 Ascension Day
May 19 Whit Monday
May 29 Corpus Christi
Nov. 1 All Saints' Day
Nov. 19 Repentance Day
Dec. 25 Christmas Day
Dec. 26 Boxing Day

ITALIAN
Jan. 1 New Year's Day
Jan. 6 Epiphany
Mar. 19 St. Joseph's Day
Mar. 31 Easter Monday
Apr. 25 Liberation Day
May 1 Labour Day
May 8 Ascension Day
May 29 Corpus Christi
Jun. 2 Italian National Day
Jun. 29 SS. Peter & Paul Day
Aug. 15 Assumption Day
Nov. 1 All Saints' Day
Nov. 4 National Unity Day
Dec. 8 Immaculate Conception Day
Dec. 25 Christmas Day
Dec. 26 Boxing Day

THINGS TO DO

1. How many holidays do you have in a year? (Remember to include weekends.) Find out the names of some of the special festivals and holidays the Romans had. Make a chart comparing your holidays with the Romans' holidays and those of people in present-day European countries. (The extract from a diary, on the left, will help you.)
2. What is the modern meaning of the word 'Circus'? How has the meaning changed? Write down your answers.
3. What are the most popular sports or entertainments today? Why do you think they are popular? Are there any sports that were popular in Roman times similar to those we know today? Are there any which you feel would not be acceptable to people today? Have a discussion in class about these questions.
4. Find out what sports are played or enjoyed by modern Heads of State, for example, the Prime Minister and the Royal Family. Are these sports popular or not? Give a reason for your answer.

2 : CHARIOT RACES

The Circus Maximus

The *Circus Maximus* (or, in English, the Great Circus) was a huge building: it was 600 metres long and 200 metres wide, and could hold 250,000 spectators. Hampden Park in Glasgow, the largest stadium in Britain, holds 150,000.

The track was roughly oval in shape, and had a barrier down the middle, called the **spina**, or backbone.

The turning-points at each end of the *spina* were marked by three conical posts, called **metae**. The chariots were released from twelve starting-gates (**carceres**, or stalls) at one end of the track. The laps were indicated by seven large wooden eggs (**ova**). The exact position of these is not known, but possibly they were on the *spina*, as shown on pages 9, 10 and 17.

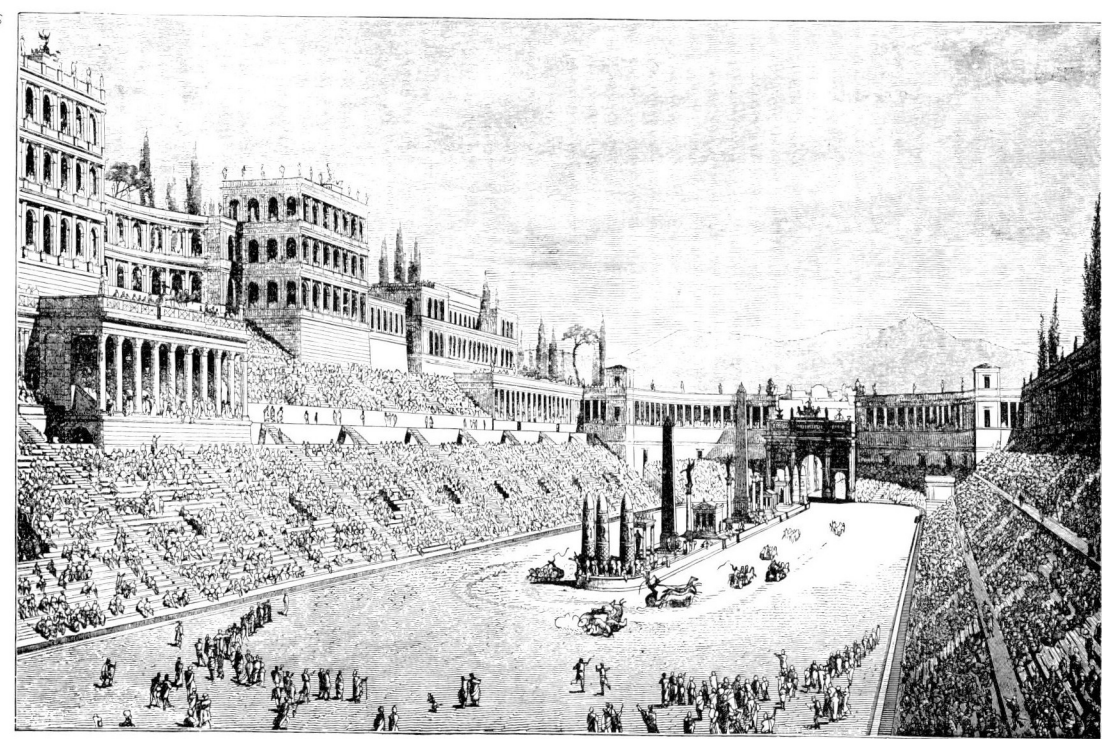

A drawing of the *Circus Maximus* (restoration)

The signal for the start of a race was the dropping of a white cloth by the President of the Games, who was often the Emperor. The chariots had to do seven laps of the track, which is about two and a half miles. The most exciting and dangerous part of the race was at the turning-points; because of the sharp turn crashes were frequent.

It was normal to have twenty-four races a day at the Circus; this is much more than modern horse-racing, at which there are usually six races in an afternoon.

On one occasion, according to Suetonius (he wrote the life-stories of the Emperors), the Emperor Domitian reduced the number of laps from seven to five, so that a hundred races a day could be run off!

A coin showing the *Circus Maximus*. Try to find the *spina, metae,* and the tall pillar in the middle of the *spina*.

Horses

Horses were run in teams of two, three, four, six or seven, though four was the most common number. All were highly trained. Some became very famous, like Tuscus, which won 386 first prizes, or Victor, which lived up to its name by winning 429 times.

The Emperor Caligula had a favourite horse called Incitatus (Swift), according to Suetonius:

> The Emperor was always worried that the horse would become nervous, so, on the day before the Races, he filled the neighbourhood with troops to ensure complete silence.
>
> Incitatus had a marble stable, an ivory stall, purple blankets, and a jewelled collar; also a house, furniture, and slaves—to entertain any guests he invited in the horse's name. It is said he even intended to make Incitatus Consul (a kind of Prime Minister).

Suetonius *Caligula* 55

The poet Martial mentions another famous horse called Andraemon:

> I am a famous poet, but not as famous as Andraemon!

Martial *Epigrams* 10.9

Horses had their own supporters, who used to back them no matter what happened, as we can see from this inscription from a public baths in North Africa:

> 'Win or lose, we love you, Polydoxus!'

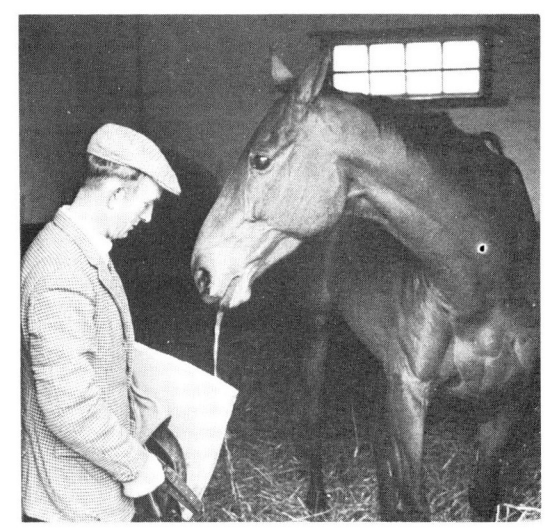

This horse, Arkle, was so famous in the 1960s that a song was written about it.

Charioteers

The charioteers earned huge sums of money, and were as glamorous as modern footballers or pop-stars. Men like Scorpus, Epaphroditus and Pompeius Musclosus had hundreds, even thousands, of victories to their credit, and were household names.

Some of them seem to have had fan-clubs: Scorpus, for example, was known by his 'golden nose', which, according to Martial, 'twinkled everywhere', that is, his many fans had pictures of him.

But their money was not won easily. Their lives, though glamorous, were also very dangerous, considering the crashes that must have happened often. Fatal accidents were common: Fuscus was killed at the age of 24 after 57 victories, Crescens at 22 after winning one and a half million sesterces (£150,000), and Marcus Aurelius Mollicius at 20 after 125 victories.

A chariot rounding the 'metae'. The driver has the reins wrapped tightly round his body for greater stability. He also carried a knife to cut himself free in case of an accident.

The charioteers were organised into four teams which were known by their different colours: the Reds, the Whites, the Blues, and the Greens. Each team had its own stables, trainers and backers, who made great profits out of their investments.

According to Suetonius, the Emperors usually supported one or other of the teams. Caligula was such an enthusiastic supporter of the Greens that he often had dinner or even spent the night at their headquarters.

Vitellius was a fan of the Blues, and once had some men executed for chanting:

'Down with the Blues!'

The Emperor Domitian added two new teams, the Purples and the Golds, but these probably did not survive his reign. The Purples are referred to in the epitaph of one of Rome's most famous charioteers, Epaphroditus:

To the departed spirit of Epaphroditus,
Charioteer of the Reds.
He won 178 prizes with the Reds.
He won 8 prizes with the Purples.
His wife, Beia Feicula, erected this in
his memory, willingly, for he deserved it.

Quite clearly, Epaphroditus was 'transferred' to the Purples, perhaps to get the new team off to a good start.

A mosaic showing a chariot race. You can see clearly all the features of the Circus:
a spectators' stand
b *carceres*
c *metae*
d *spina*
e *ova*

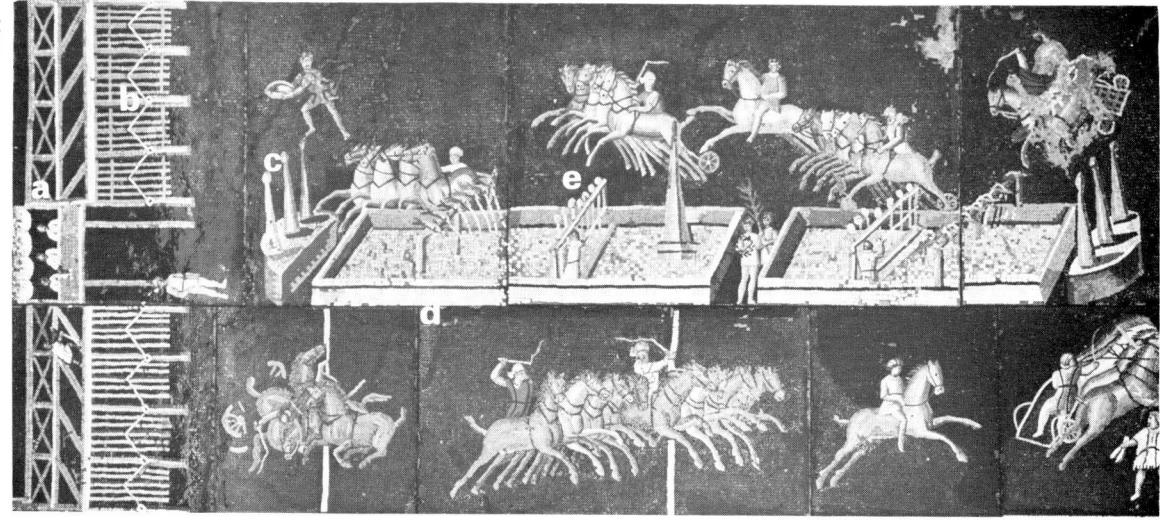

Diocles

The most successful drivers made a great deal of money. Here is an inscription dedicated to a man who was probably Rome's most famous charioteer, Diocles:

Gaius Apuleius Diocles, Charioteer of the Reds, a Spaniard, aged 42 years, 7 months, and 23 days. He drove his first chariot with the Whites in AD 122. He won his first victory with the same team shortly after. His first victory with the Reds was in AD 131.

Grand totals: he drove chariots for 24 years, started in 4,257 races and won 1,462 of them.

He won 92 major money prizes, made up as follows:
32 prizes worth 30,000 sesterces (£3,000)
28 prizes worth 40,000 sesterces (£4,000)
29 prizes worth 50,000 sesterces (£5,000)
 3 prizes worth 60,000 sesterces (£6,000)
In all, he won a total of 35,863,120 sesterces (£3$\frac{1}{2}$ million).

Charioteers (from a relief)

A Day at the Races

All Rome is today at the Circus; these shows are for young men, who like to shout and swagger and make bets with their girl-friends at their side.

Juvenal *Satires* 11.197

This is how the poet Juvenal describes the atmosphere at the Circus. People came from far and near to see the races; to all of them it was an exciting and colourful spectacle. Some liked to make bets, while others, especially women, were there because it was a big social event, and not to be missed.

The races started with a procession of chariots through the Processional Gate, the horses sleek and well-groomed, the charioteers splendid in their colourful costumes. To add to it all, statues of gods and goddesses were paraded: Jupiter, King of the Gods, Mars, God of War, Venus, Goddess of Love and Beauty, and Neptune, the patron God of Horses. The people in the crowd wore the colours of their favourites: red, white, blue or green, according to the wearer's fancy.

Chariot race from the film *Ben Hur*: the parade

Sometimes, when there was a big crowd, it was uncomfortably hot and cramped in the seats. The poet Ovid describes the scene (he is there with his girl-friend):

You on the right, sir—please be careful,
Your elbow's hurting the lady.

And you in the row behind—sit up, sir!
Your knees are digging into her back.

But what about a breath of air while we wait?
This programme will do as a fan.

At one point, Ovid imagines that he is the charioteer his girl-friend is cheering for:

How I envy your charioteer!
He's a lucky man to be picked by you.

I wish it was me. I'd get my team
off to a flying start,

crack the whip, give them their heads
and shave the post with my nearside wheel.

But if I caught sight of *you* in the race
I'd drop the reins and lose ground.

Ovid then describes the race:

Now they've cleared the course. The Praetor's starting the
 first race.
Four-horse chariots. Look—they're off.

There's your driver. Anyone *you* back is bound to win.
Even the horses seem to know what you want.

My God, he's taking the corner too wide.
What are you doing? The man behind is drawing level.

What are you doing, wretch? Breaking a poor girl's heart.
For pity's sake pull on your left rein!

We've backed a loser. Come on everyone, all together,
flap your togas and signal a fresh start.

Now, they're off again—plunging out of the stalls,
rushing down the course in a clash of colours.

Now's your chance to take the lead. Go all out for that gap.
Give my girl and me what we want.

Hurrah, he's done it! You've got what you wanted,
 sweetheart.
That only leaves me—do I win too?

She's smiling. There's a promise in those bright eyes.
Let's leave now. You can pay my bet in private.

Ovid *Amores* 3.2 (from a translation by Guy Lee, published by John Murray)

Chariot race from *Ben Hur*: the race

Ben Hur

Here is a description of the exciting finish of a chariot race. The two chief drivers are Ben Hur, a Jew, and Messala, a Roman, who are sworn enemies of each other. The other drivers are Lysippus of Corinth, Dicaeus of Byzantium, and Admetus of Sidon. It takes place in the Circus at Antioch in Syria. At this point in the race, Messala is leading and Ben Hur is second.

. . . Messala was just moving round the turning-point. To pass him, Ben Hur had to cross the track, and take the inside position. The thousands on the benches understood it all. They saw the signal given—the magnificent response; the team close outside Messala's offside wheel; Ben Hur's nearside wheel behind the other's chariot—all this they saw.

Then they heard a crash loud enough to send a thrill through the Circus, and, quicker than thought, out over the course a spray of shining white and yellow cinders flew. Down on its right side toppled the Roman's chariot. There was a rebound as of the axle hitting the hard earth, another and another. Then the chariot went to pieces, and Messala, entangled in the reins, pitched forward headlong.

Chariot race from *Ben Hur*: the crash

To increase the horror, the Sidonian, who had the inside behind him, could not stop or turn out. Into the wreck he drove at full speed; then over the Roman, and into his team, all mad with fear. Presently, out of the turmoil, the struggling of horses, the murky cloud of dust and sand, he crawled, just in time to see the others go down the track after Ben Hur, who now held the lead.

The people arose, and leaped upon the benches and shouted and screamed. Those who looked that way caught glimpses of Messala, now under the abandoned chariots. He was still; they thought him dead; but everyone else followed Ben Hur in his dash for the finish.

They had not seen the cunning touch of the reins by which he caught Messala's wheels with the iron-shod point of his axle, and crushed it; but they had seen the change in the man, and felt the heat and glow of his spirit, and the way he had so suddenly inspired his Arab stallions.

And such running! When the Byzantine and Corinthian were half-way down the course, Ben Hur passed the line.

And the race was won!

Lew Wallace *Ben Hur*

Chariot race from *Ben Hur:* crowd scene

A different view

Not everyone enjoyed the Circus Games. Here is another point of view:

The Circus Games don't interest me in the slightest. There's nothing new or different about them; if you've seen one race, you've seen them all.

I just can't understand why so many thousands of people want to see again and again (it's so childish!) horses racing and men driving chariots.

It wouldn't be so bad if they appreciated the horses' speed or the drivers' skill. But all they see is the colour of the tunic. If you swapped over the colours, I'm quite sure they wouldn't notice the difference.

And it's not just the masses who are obsessed with chariot racing, but some sensible and important men, too.

In my opinion it's a completely useless way of spending the time

Pliny the Younger 9.6

Make a list of the features marked **a-g**

QUESTIONS

1. How big was the Circus and how many could it hold? (page 5)
2. What were
   a. the *spina*
   b. the *metae*
   c. the *carceres*
   d. the *ova*? (page 5)
3. How many laps were in a race? What was the distance of a race? How many races were there usually in a day? (page 6)
4. Name
   a. three famous horses
   b. three famous charioteers (pages 7 and 8)
5. What were
   a. the advantages
   b. the disadvantages of a charioteer's life? (page 8)
6. Name the four teams. What two were added later and by whom? (page 9)
7. Why do you think the races were so popular? (pages 10 and 11)
8. Why do you think women enjoyed the races? (page 11)
9. How many drivers are mentioned in the chariot race described by Ovid? How many in *Ben Hur*? (pages 12 and 14)
10. Why does the writer on page 16 think chariot races a waste of time?

THINGS TO DO

1. Draw a ground plan of the Circus Maximus. (see page 5)
2. Draw a scene from a chariot race.
3. Write a newspaper article (with headlines) describing the accidental deaths of *one* of the charioteers on page 8.
4. Write an obituary of EITHER Epaphroditus OR Scorpus.
5. Describe, in your own words, what happened in the race on page 12.
6. Write a newspaper article (with headlines) describing the race from *Ben Hur* on pages 14 and 15.
7. Do you agree or not with the writer on page 16 when he says:
   'If you've seen one race (or football match), you've seen them all.' Write a reply to the writer giving him your opinion.
   Give some reasons for your opinion.
8. Do you think that sport is a waste of time or not? Divide into two groups—one in favour of sport and one against—and organise a class discussion.

3 : AMPHITHEATRES

The word 'amphitheatre' means 'double theatre'. A Roman theatre was shaped like the letter D. If you imagine two Ds back to back with the uprights taken away, then you get an oval shape. And that was the shape of an amphitheatre. (Sometimes it was more round than this.)

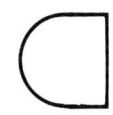

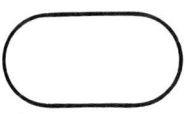

The stadium consisted of a sand-covered arena, surrounded by banked tiers (rows) of seats.

The shows presented in the Roman arenas were of many different kinds, but usually involved gladiators and wild animals.

A large number of amphitheatres were built all over the Roman Empire, and some of these can still be seen today.

The one shown in the picture is at Nîmes in the south of France, and is very well preserved; in its heyday it could seat 25,000 spectators.

As you can see, it is still used today for bull fights; bulls were probably killed here in Roman times as well.

The Romans built some amphitheatres in Britain as well, and you can still see one of them. It is in Wales, in the village of Caerleon, near Newport, in Monmouthshire, which was the site of a large Roman legionary fort.

The amphitheatre at Caerleon was built in the second half of the first century AD. It was just outside the fort, and was probably used for military parades as well as for public entertainment. The arena was oval, and surrounded by eight sections of spectators' seats. It could hold about 6,000 people.

An aerial view of the amphitheatre at Caerleon

This is what it looked like in Roman times

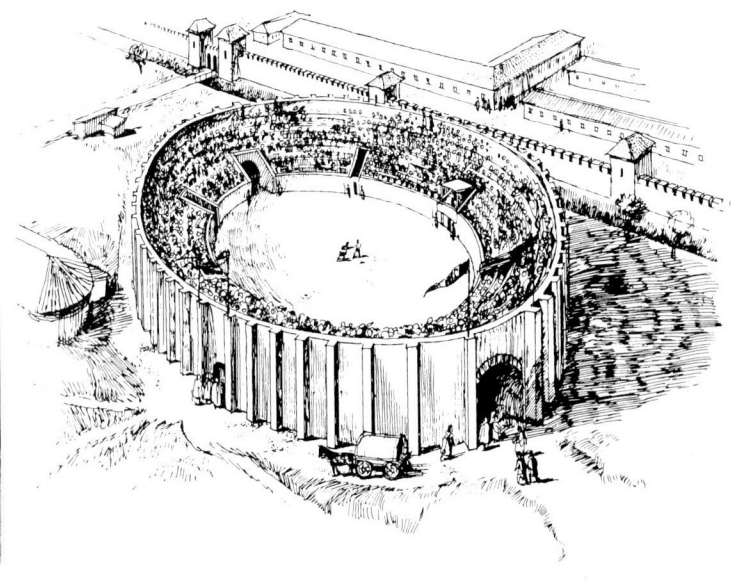

The Colosseum

The most famous amphitheatre anywhere in the world is the Colosseum in Rome, which was also built in the first century AD, by the Emperors Vespasian and Titus. It was originally called the Flavian Amphitheatre, after the family name, Flavius, of the two emperors. But it got its present name from a huge statue, or Colossus, of Nero, which stood nearby. This was such a well known landmark in Rome that its name survived even after the statue was removed and later destroyed. Then the amphitheatre became known as the Colosseum—'the amphitheatre near the Colossus'.

You can just see the Colossus in the picture on the right, it showed Nero as the sun-god and was over 30 metres high.

Reconstruction of the Colosseum showing the Colossus

The Colosseum could hold 50,000 spectators, 45,000 of them seated. There were eighty entrance arches on the outside of the building. In the picture below, gate **A** and another on the opposite side were used by the Emperor and his guests. Gate **B** is the performers' entrance to the arena, while gate **C** had a more sinister purpose: it was used for dragging out dead bodies, both animal and human. **D** is the arena, which was covered with sand, and **E** is where the spectators sat.

The other gates were numbered from 1 to 76, though only thirty of these survive (nos. 23 to 54). Tickets were distributed before each show; all that the holder had to do was to go to the gate marked on his ticket. The large number of gates meant that there was hardly any crush at the beginning or end of a show.

A cutaway drawing of the Colosseum as it was in Roman times

The bottom row of seats was reserved for Roman senators, and the rows behind for middle class citizens. Behind them sat the lower classes, then foreigners, then finally, furthest away from the arena, slaves.

The best seat of all, of course, was the Imperial Box, where the Emperor and his guests sat; it was fitted with a secret underground passageway, which the Emperor could use in an emergency.

The Emperor Augustus laid down the following rules: soldiers sat apart from civilians; special seats were reserved for married couples and for boys and their tutors; dark clothes were banned, except in the back rows. He also at one point separated men from women: the women had to sit at the back; the only exceptions to this were the priestesses of Vesta, who had their own box beside the Emperor's (see next page).

Today the Colosseum is a bare shadow of what it used to be. There is hardly a trace left of the marble seats which once used to be there. During the Middle Ages it became a vast quarry, and was stripped bare by Romans wanting marble for their houses and palaces.

The arena has also lost its surface. This happened when the Roman City Council decided at the beginning of this century to lay bare the underground passages, where the animals were kept. As a result, what you see now is an amphitheatre without seats or arena.

And yet, the Colosseum remains the symbol of Rome. The Venerable Bede, one of the early Christians in the seventh century AD, wrote these famous words of it:

As long as the Colosseum stands, Rome will stand.
When the Colosseum falls, Rome will fall.
When Rome falls, the world will fall.

a the arena
b the emperor's box
c spectators' seats

QUESTIONS

1. What does the word 'amphitheatre' mean? What shape was the arena? (page 19)
2. What shows were held at Caerleon Amphitheatre? (page 20)
3. Who built the Colosseum? What was its original name? What was the Colossus? What does the word 'colosseum' mean? (page 21)
4. How many spectators could the Colosseum hold? How many gates were there? Which of these were barred to the public and why? Why were so many gates necessary? (page 22)
5. What classes of people had different seats and in what order did they sit? (page 23)
6. How did the Colosseum lose (a) its seats (b) the surface of the arena? (page 24)

THINGS TO DO

1. Make a drawing of the outside of the Colosseum and label the gates. Draw a plan of the inside showing where the various people sat.
2. Find out the names of other Roman amphitheatres. Look at your atlases to find out where they are. Are any still in use today and what kinds of entertainments are held there?
3. Compare the gate system of the Colosseum with that of any modern stadium. Make a table showing the differences.
4. What are the seating arrangements in a modern (a) football stadium (b) cinema (c) theatre? Draw plans to illustrate your answers.
5. Look at page 23. Why do you think Augustus laid down these rules? (Think about each one.) Design a notice for the outside of the Colosseum giving details of the rules about the seating.

Coin showing a fight between a bull and an elephant in the Colosseum. On the left is the Colossus

4 : GLADIATORS

Two shows

```
            AT POMPEII           APRIL 8TH-12TH
        20 PAIRS OF GLADIATORS WILL FIGHT IN COMBAT
            THE PROPERTY OF LUCRETIUS SATRIUS VALENS
            LIFE-PRIEST OF THE EMPEROR NERO CAESAR
                             PLUS
                    10 PAIRS OF GLADIATORS
            THE PROPERTY OF LUCRETIUS SON OF VALENS
                             PLUS
                   FULL-SCALE ANIMAL HUNTS
                A SUN-SHADE WILL BE PROVIDED
```

This advertisement appears, written in red letters, on the wall of a house in Pompeii. The show is typical of the small ones held all over the Roman Empire.

At the opposite end of the scale were the shows held in Rome. In AD 116 the Emperor Trajan celebrated his conquest of Dacia (modern Roumania) with a show which lasted nearly four months! During this show 4,941 pairs of gladiators fought in the arena.

Bust of the Emperor Trajan

Spartacus

At first, gladiators (the word means swordsmen) were soldiers who fought as part of a funeral ceremony for dead heroes. Later, as gladiator shows became popular entertainment, they were recruited from tough slaves and prisoners-of-war. They were kept chained up in barracks called 'schools', and were often treated very cruelly.

In 73 BC some gladiators in Capua (in the south of Italy) rebelled against this treatment and escaped, led by a man called **Spartacus**. Thousands of slaves and peasants joined them, and for two whole years they roamed wildly through Italy, burning and looting.

Despite several successes against the Roman legions, they were eventually beaten and Spartacus was killed, fighting bravely at the head of his men. But his companions were not so lucky. Six thousand of them were taken prisoner and strung up on crosses all the way along the road from Rome to Capua.

The story of Spartacus has been made into a film, which you may have seen, starring Kirk Douglas.

Spartacus and his men fighting a Roman legion

Types of gladiators and their equipment

Gladiators were named according to their equipment. Originally this was armour connected with their home countries: **Thracians** from Thrace (modern Bulgaria), **Gauls** from Gaul (modern France), and **Samnites** from Samnium (central Italy). These three types all had helmet, breast-plate and greaves (leg-pieces).

The Thracian seems to have been more lightly-armed, and had a round shield and curved dagger.

The Gaul (sometimes called **Myrmillo**) had a sword and shield, and was distinguished by the image of a fish or sea-creature on his helmet.

The most heavily-armed gladiator was the Samnite, who was covered from head to toe, and had a large rectangular shield and an axe.

All three types were called **secutors** (or pursuers) when they were set against the lightly-armed **retiarius** (or net-fighter) who carried a net, trident, dagger and shoulder-guard.

A mosaic showing gladiators in the arena. Find a *secutor*, a *retiarius* and a Gaul.

The reason for the *retiarius's* strange equipment is not known, but it is referred to in a popular song of the day (the words are spoken by a *retiarius* to a Gaul):

Why run away from me, Gaul?
It's not you I'm after at all—
It's your fish!

The contest between the *secutor* and the *retiarius* was always the most popular with the crowd because of the contrast in the amount of armour they carried and the big differences between them. The *secutor,* heavily-armed and always on the attack, represented brute force, while the *retiarius,* lightly-armed and always on the retreat, represented skill and cunning, which the crowd greatly admired.

The picture below is a mosaic from a Roman villa in Sussex. It shows the *secutor* and *retiarius* at different stages of the fight, accompanied by a trainer. The gladiators are shown as 'cupids', that is, they all have wings.

Mosaic of Cupid gladiators
from Bignor Villa, in Sussex

The salute

Before the show began, all the gladiators had to submit their weapons to an official, often the Emperor himself, for inspection; only the sharpest blades were kept.

The first part of the show was a parade of the combatants, who walked around amid the cheers of the crowd. Then came a solemn moment as the gladiators halted in front of the Emperor's box, raised their weapons and spoke the familiar words:

'Hail, Caesar, we salute you, we who are about to die.'

Then they paired off according to the draw, and the show began.

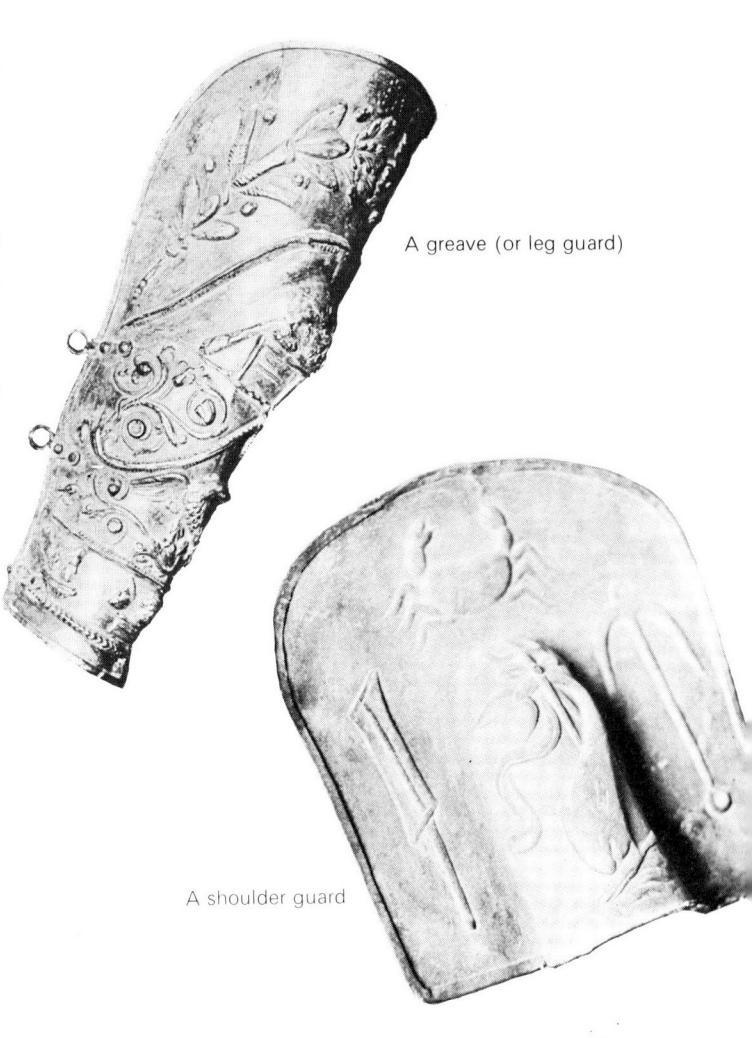

A greave (or leg guard)

A gladiator's helmet

A shoulder guard

This is a famous mosaic showing a gladiator combat. There are two separate fights going on. On the left, a *retiarius* called Alumnus has just killed a Samnite called Mazicinus, who lies on the ground with his shield over him. The word VIC beside Alumnus' name means victor or winner.

On the right, a *secutor* whose name is missing has defeated a *retiarius* called Callimorfus. The beaten gladiator is making an appeal for mercy. The small figure at the top of the picture is probably an instructor or referee about to make his decision (R = *rector*). In the bottom right hand corner, the artist has included a beast-fighter, called Serpentius, fighting a leopard.

A mosaic showing a gladiator and a *bestiarius* (see page 43)

A question of thumbs

Gladiators usually fought to the death, but sometimes the defeated man was spared, if he had fought well. First, he had to 'appeal to the finger', that is, he held up a finger, admitting defeat and asking for mercy.

If he was successful, the crowd gave the 'thumbs pressed' sign, and he walked away alive; if not, they gave the 'thumbs turned' sign, and the wretched man was killed, amidst a fanfare of trumpets.

The exact meaning of the phrases, 'thumbs pressed' and 'thumbs turned' is not certain. The thumb probably represented the sword; to turn the thumb was to whirl and use it, and to press the thumb was to put it back in its sheath.

The modern phrases 'thumbs up' and 'thumbs down' meaning good and bad, are based on a misunderstanding of the phrases above.

The 'appeal to the finger' (from a terracotta vase)
The gladiators' names are given: on the left, a Secutor called Memnon, and on the right, a Retiarius called Valentinus.

Another sign of mercy was the waving of handkerchiefs by the crowd. Martial tells the story of Hermogenes, whose weakness was stealing handkerchiefs:

Once, in the amphitheatre, the gladiator Myrinus was wounded and asked to be spared. The crowd waved their handkerchiefs in the air in his favour, and when some of these fell on to the arena, Hermogenes ran out and stole four!

Martial *Epigrams* 12.29

One gladiator, whose name we do not know, once made the fatal mistake of sparing an opponent's life. Then the two met again, and this time he was beaten and killed by the man he had spared.
This is his epitaph:
'Take my advice, when you fight in a show,
If you beat your opponent, don't let him go!'

The death of a fallen gladiator (from a relief)

The wooden sword

Martial has another story of two gladiators called Priscus and Verus who fought till they were exhausted, with neither man winning or likely to win. The crowd had enjoyed the fight, and shouted for them both to be spared. The Emperor (Domitian) found a simple solution to this draw: both were declared winners, and both received the wooden sword and palm of victory.

The wooden sword was presented to gladiators who had fought long and well, and meant two things: if a man was a slave, he became free, and if he was free, he could retire from the arena.

A veteran fighter called Flamma received the wooden sword four times in his career, but on each occasion he signed on again; perhaps because he missed the life or the money, or both.

A drawing of a gladiator appealing for his life

Champions and heart-throbs

Gladiators were greatly admired for their strength and bravery in the face of death. Many inscriptions, from all over the Empire, point to their popularity, especially with women.

Here is one from Leicester:

'Verecunda (Modesty), actress, loves Lucius, gladiator.' And another from Pompeii:

'Celadus, the Thracian gladiator, is the girls' heart-throb.'

The poet Martial wrote a whole poem about another one, called Hermes:

Hermes, champion fighter of the century,
Hermes, skilled in the use of all arms,
Hermes, both gladiator and trainer,
Hermes, the scourge and terror of the shows,
Hermes, feared alone by Helius and Advolans,
Hermes, trained to win, but not to kill,
Hermes, always a sell-out when he appears,
Hermes, darling of the actresses,
Hermes, arrogant with deadly spear,
Hermes, menacing with Neptune's trident,
Hermes, terrifying in crested helmet,
Hermes, glory of Mars, three in one.

Martial *Epigrams* 5.24

Inscription of Lucius and Verecunda

Riot at Pompeii

'Long live the Nucerians!
Death to the Pompeians!'

This is an inscription written on the wall of a house in Pompeii. It describes the rivalry between Pompeii and the neighbouring town of Nuceria, which led to a riot in AD 59.

It all started at a gladiator show given by Livineius Regulus and attended by supporters from both towns, in the amphitheatre at Pompeii. Something happened (nobody knows what) during the show which caused the two groups to start insulting each other. Then things got rapidly worse when stones were thrown and before long, swords and daggers were drawn.

The Pompeians, who were more in number, soon got the upper hand and the Nucerians were overwhelmed. Troops had to be called in, and when order was finally restored,

This is a painting of the riot, made by an eye-witness.

the amphitheatre and streets were littered with dead and wounded.

After it was all over, the Town Council of Nuceria made a claim for damages against the Pompeians, in whose town the show had been held, and they appealed to the Emperor (Nero) in Rome.

An investigation was held, and both sides went to the capital to plead their cases; many of the wounded Nucerians were taken to appear personally. After careful consideration of the facts, the court found in favour of the Nucerians, and Pompeii was barred from having such shows for the next ten years. Regulus, the organiser, was convicted and exiled, along with the men who had been ringleaders in the riot.

This is the entrance staircase of the amphitheatre at Pompeii. You can see it clearly in the painting on page 36

The taste of blood

Once the writer Seneca saw a really vicious type of show, but what struck him most was the crowd's attitude:

Once I happened to go to the Midday Games, expecting to see some light entertainment, or at least something different from the usual bloodshed. It was the exact opposite; the other shows were a picnic in comparison. This was pure murder, and in dead earnest.

When one man falls, another immediately takes his place. And this goes on and on, till none are left, for even the last man is killed.

You may say, 'But that one committed a robbery.'
So what? Does he deserve to be crucified?
'He committed murder.'
Even so, does he deserve to die like this? What sort of punishment do you deserve, you wretch, for watching him?

All day long the crowd cries, 'Kill him, flog him, burn him! Why does he run on to the sword so timidly? Why is he so unwilling to die?'

Seneca *Letters* 1.7

A modern drawing of gladiators fighting it out

The story of Alypius

St. Augustine, a great Christian writer of about AD 400, tells the story of Alypius:

Alypius had gone to Rome to study law. One day he met some friends of his in the street, who were going to the amphitheatre. Despite his protests, they dragged him along with them. Alypius kept shouting, 'You can drag my body to that place, but you can't make my mind and eyes watch those shows!'

When they reached the amphitheatre, they went in and managed to find some seats. Alypius shut his eyes and kept trying to concentrate on something else. But the noise of the crowd was too much for him, and, overcome by curiosity, he opened his eyes.

The wound he received in his soul was far more severe than any gladiator received in his body. When he saw the blood, he couldn't turn away but kept his eyes on it. He was delighted by the cruelty and frenzy; he was almost drunk with the pleasure of seeing blood spilt.

Need I say more? He watched, he shouted, he raged with excitement. In the end, he became a more devoted fan of the shows than any of his companions.

St. Augustine *Confessions* 6.8

Wall painting from Pompeii of gladiators

QUESTIONS

1. How many gladiators were in (a) the show at Pompeii (b) Trajan's show?
   How long did each show last? (page 26)
2. What sorts of men usually became gladiators?
   Where were they kept and how were they treated?
   What happened to Spartacus and his men—in the end? (page 27)
3. What countries did the gladiators originally come from? What equipment was worn by (a) the Thracian (b) the Gaul/*Myrmillo* (c) the Samnite (d) the *retiarius*? What was the *secutor*? (page 28)
4. What was the inspection for?
   What did the gladiators say to the Emperor? (page 30)
5. What was the 'appeal to the finger'?
   What is the likely meaning of 'thumbs turned' and 'thumbs pressed'? (page 32)
6. Why was the wooden sword given to some gladiators? What did it mean? (page 34)
7. Look at page 38.
   a What was different about this show?
   b What did Seneca think of the crowd?
8. What made Alypius change his mind about gladiator shows? (page 39)

THINGS TO DO

1. Describe a day in the life of a gladiator.
2. Make a radio commentary on a fight involving EITHER Hermes OR Priscus and Verus. This could be taped.
3. It is your first visit to a gladiator show. Write what you see and think.
4. Draw a scene involving a *secutor* and a *retiarius*.
5. Imagine that you are interviewing Flamma on the occasion of his fourth wooden sword. Give his reasons for signing on again.
6. Describe everything you can see in the picture on page 36.
7. Imagine you are a reporter sent from Rome to cover the riot described on pages 36 and 37. You arrive the day after; you interview both sides to discover what happened. Write down the article you then send to your editor.
8. Discuss in class: 'Crowd violence'. Why do crowds behave like this? What can be done to prevent it happening?

5: ANIMAL HUNTS AND SEA FIGHTS

Animals for public shows were big business in ancient Rome. The public's appetite for animal hunts and acts was enormous, and the supply of animals was a profitable trade. The Empire was searched for wild and exotic animals and no expense was spared; the most sought after animals were lions, boars, bulls, bears and elephants, though almost every known species was hunted.

This is a letter written by Cicero, the governor of Cilicia (a Roman province in Asia Minor), to Caelius, a magistrate in Rome who had asked him to supply certain animals:

My dear Caelius,
About the panthers—the hunters are doing everything possible, on my instructions. But there is a shortage; the ones that are still there are said to be complaining that they are the only living creatures being hunted in the province. And so, according to rumour, they've decided to leave this province and emigrate to Caria.
And yet the hunters are doing their best, especially Patiscus. Whatever turns up will be yours, but I won't make any rash promises.

Yours,
Cicero.

Cicero *Ad Familiares* 2.11

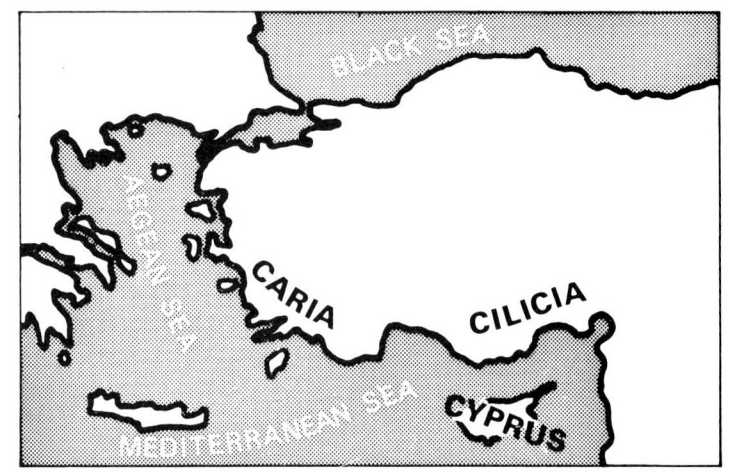

Map of Asia Minor showing Cilicia and Caria

A mosaic showing a boar being hunted by a horseman and his dog

Performing animals

The Emperor Augustus used to put the more exotic animals on exhibition: a rhinoceros in the *Campus Martius* (a public park), a tiger on the stage of the Theatre, and a snake nearly 28 metres long in the *Forum* (City Centre).

Performing animals were very popular. Martial describes a famous occasion:

In the arena we have seen a leopard with a yoke on his spotted neck, and furious tigers enduring patiently the blows of a whip; stags and bears with a golden bit; a huge boar with a purple muzzle; buffaloes dragging chariots and an elephant dancing for his swarthy trainer.

And yet this is nothing compared with the lions in pursuit of hares. They catch them, let them go, then catch them again; the hares are safer in the lions' mouths than anywhere else. The lions are ashamed to harm them, for they have just come from killing bulls.

Martial *Epigrams* 1.104

A mosaic from St Albans showing a lion with a stag's head in its mouth

Another mosaic. What animals can you see?

Beast fighters

The 'entertainment' in a Roman animal show was a hunt to the death—either of animals by other animals, or of animals by trained hunters called **Bestiarii** or Beast Fighters.

One of the most famous beast fighters was Carpophorus, who once killed a bear, a lion and a leopard single-handed. Even women were known to fight animals in the arena; Juvenal describes one called Maevia, who 'bare-breasted, brandished a hunting-spear and pierced a Tuscan boar.'

One or two of the Emperors occasionally appeared in the arena to fight animals, but the contest was hardly equal. According to Suetonius, Nero once 'had a lion drugged so that he could safely face it before the entire amphitheatre, and then either kill it with his club or strangle it'.

The Emperor Commodus was an excellent archer, and used to shoot arrows into a pack of lions from the safety of the Imperial Box.

This fight seems to be taking place in the Circus (notice the seven eggs you read about on page 5). Notice also the spectators on the left

The slaughter of animals

The number of animals killed in the Roman amphitheatres is almost unbelievable. The Emperor Augustus boasted of having had 3,500 animals killed in his shows. Seventy years later, Titus had 5,000 killed in a single day!

In AD 249 the Emperor Philip held spectacular games to celebrate the thousandth anniversary of the founding of Rome (753 BC). All the animals in Rome at the time were killed: 32 elephants, 10 elks, 10 tigers, 60 tame lions, 30 tame leopards, 10 hyenas, 6 hippos, 1 rhinoceros, 10 zebra, 10 giraffes, 20 wild asses, and 40 wild horses.

Men against beasts and on the left, beasts against men

It is easy to believe that the Romans were a cruel and vicious race. Certainly they were passionately fond of gladiator and animal shows with all their brutal killing. But occasionally we hear a voice of protest. This is another letter of Cicero's, in which he describes Pompey's Games:

The remaining five days were taken up with animal hunts, which were certainly splendid. But what civilised man can enjoy the sight of a feeble man being mauled by a powerful beast, or a noble beast being pierced by a spear? And yet, if these things must be seen, you have seen them often; we who watch them have seen nothing new.

On the last day, it was the turn of the elephants. As usual, the crowd was astonished at the sight of them, but I couldn't say I enjoyed it. They seem to be almost like human beings.

Cicero *Ad Familiares* 7.1.

Sea fights

Another popular entertainment was the **Naumachia**, or sea fight. Julius Caesar was among the first to stage one:

It was fought on an artificial lake, between Tyrian (from Tyre, in Phoenicia—modern Lebanon) and Egyptian ships, with two, three or four banks of oars, and heavily-manned.

Suetonius *Caesar* 38

These fights only took place on special occasions, because a great deal of preparation was needed to make the arena watertight; about five feet of water was needed to make the ships float. In the Colosseum, especially, the many openings made this very difficult, and there were no sea fights in it after the first century AD.

Martial, however, was at one of the Colosseum fights and wrote this poem:

You, spectator, just arrived from a far-off land,
To see our spectacular shows,
Don't be deceived when sea battles appear
And waves as if on the rolling sea.
That sea was land only a few moments ago—
You don't believe me? Just wait a little while,
Till the ships have ceased to fight, the waves to flow,
Then you will say, 'That was sea not long ago.'

Martial *Liber Spectaculorum* 24

Another very famous sea fight took place in AD 52. It was staged by the Emperor Claudius to celebrate the building of a tunnel through a mountain between the Fucine Lake (about 70 miles east of Rome) and the River Liris. It is described by Tacitus:

To enable a large crowd to see the opening ceremony, Claudius staged a sea fight in the lake itself. He provided warships manned by 19,000 men, and to prevent them escaping, he surrounded them with a circle of rafts. There was still enough space left for rowing, steering and ramming. The Praetorian Guard (the Emperor's personal body-guard) was stationed on the rafts, and other units behind ramparts from which they could fire catapults.

The coast and hillsides were thronged with spectators, who had come from as far as Rome to see the show. Claudius presided in a splendid military cloak, with the Empress Agrippina at his side in a golden dress. The fighters, who were mainly criminals, fought bravely and the survivors were spared.

After the display, the waterway was opened. But soon it was clear that it had been carelessly built; the channel was not deep enough and had to be widened. A second crowd was assembled. This time, to everyone's horror, the force of the torrent carried away everything in sight. The crash and roar caused shock and terror over a wide area.

Tacitus *Annals* 12.56

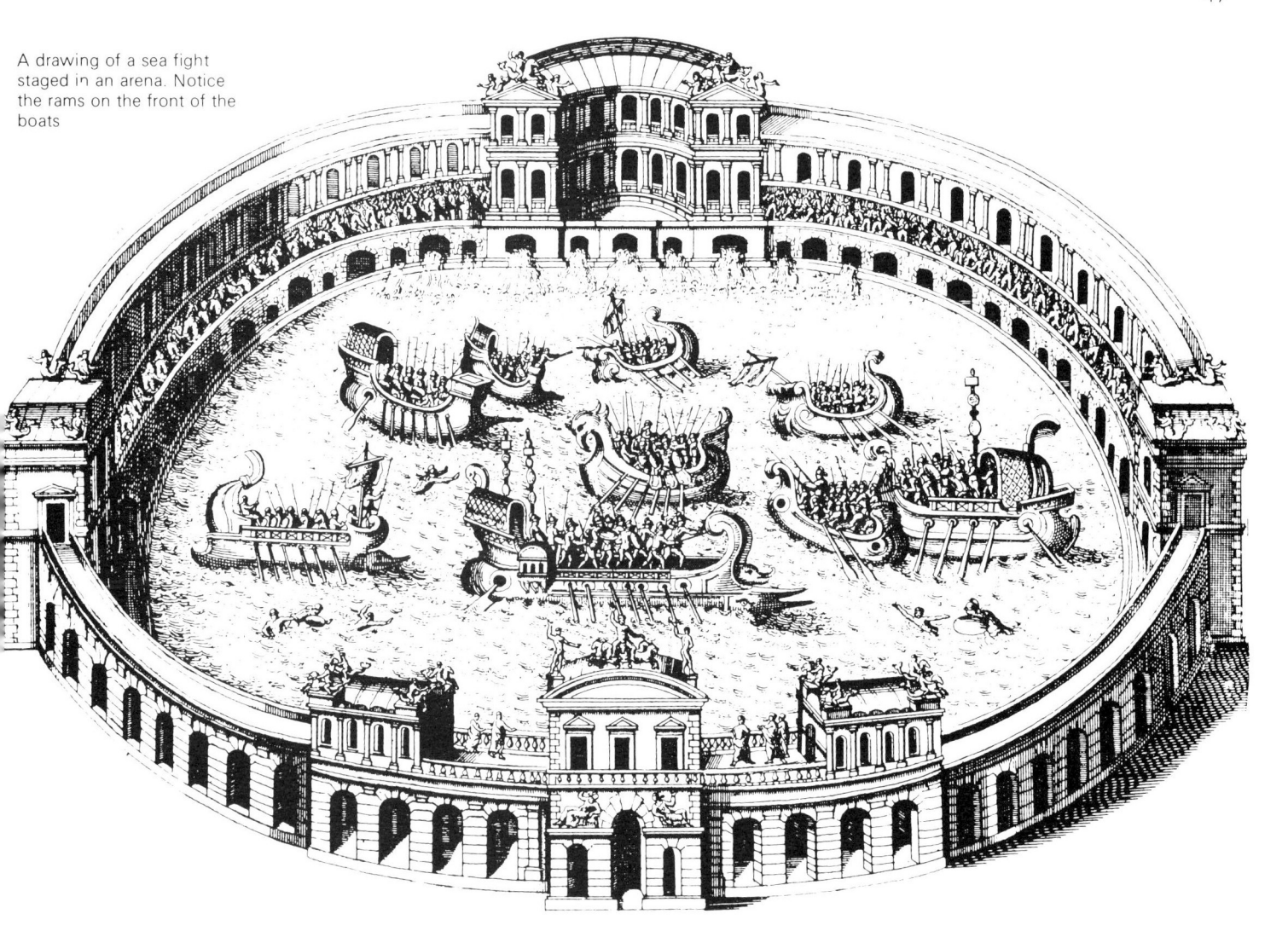

A drawing of a sea fight staged in an arena. Notice the rams on the front of the boats

QUESTIONS

1 What animals were most in demand? Why do you think this was so? (page 41)
2 Why was there a shortage of panthers in Cilicia? (page 41)
3 What kinds of animals does Martial mention? What kinds of tricks were they made to do? (page 42)
4 Who were Carpophorus and Maevia? (page 43)
5 Which emperors went in for fighting wild beasts? How did they make sure they never got hurt? (page 43)
6 How many animals were killed in the 1000th anniversary celebrations in AD 249? (page 44)
7 Why does Cicero dislike watching the slaughter of wild animals? (page 45)
8 Why did very few sea fights take place in the Colosseum? (page 46)

THINGS TO DO

1 Write a letter to a friend describing your first visit to an animal hunt.
2 Write a letter to the *Rome Daily News* complaining about the slaughter of animals in the Colosseum.
3 Write a radio commentary describing a performance by EITHER Carpophorus OR Maevia.
4 Class debate: Should we allow blood-sports in modern Britain?
5 Draw a sea fight in the Colosseum.
6 Write a newspaper article (with headlines) describing the incident on page 47.
Remember to use your own words and try to imagine the following details: extent of damage to property and persons, rescue operations, who was to blame etc.

Statue of a wild boar being attacked by dogs

6: THEATRES

The Roman theatre was copied from the Greeks, who originated the buildings, scenery, costumes and plots; all the Romans did was to make improvements. Most of the 70 theatres built by the Greeks survive in the form they were in when the Romans had finished with them, but one very good example of an original Greek theatre is at Epidavros, in Greece, pictured below.

As you can see, it is a large, open-air building, semi-circular, and with rising tiers of seats; when full, it held 18,000 spectators, which is much more than a modern theatre.

On the lowest level is a circular space called the **orchestra**, where the chorus danced and sang, and behind that the **stage** and **stage buildings.**

In the centre of the *orchestra* is the base of an altar to Dionysus, the god of music and drama.

Theatre of Orange

The Romans made several important changes in the theatre buildings. First, they made them of stone, not of wood; next, they cut down the size of the *orchestra*, and, third, they greatly enlarged the stage and stage buildings.

The Roman theatre at Orange, in the south of France, is the finest and best preserved from Roman times. It was built in the first century BC, in the reign of Augustus, and the **auditorium** (rows of seats) is set into a hillside.

The magnificent stage wall, which is 103 metres long and 38 metres high, was called by Louis XIV, a famous seventeenth-century French king, 'the finest wall in my kingdom'.

The theatre's acoustics are excellent; every sound made on the stage can be easily heard in the highest row of the auditorium.

Notice also the statue of the Emperor Augustus (over three metres high) in its special niche in the stage wall.

The theatre is still used for musical and theatrical performances

THEATRE ANTIQUE D'ORANGE
CHORÉGIE
Lundi 28 Juillet
CHŒURS ET DANSES
Prix : 5 Francs

Timbre payé sur état
N° 00243

Theatre of St Albans

The only Roman theatre left in Britain is in the Roman town of **Verulamium** (St Albans—about 25 miles north of London, in Hertfordshire), and was built in AD 155.

The seats, made of wood, were arranged in four sections round the semi-circular *orchestra*; the stage, of which only one pillar and the foundations remain, is quite small. While the plays were being presented, the *orchestra* was used to provide extra seats, probably for important citizens, such as magistrates and priests.

But the *orchestra* was also used for religious ceremonies, and probably also as an arena for bear-baiting, bull-fighting, wrestling and the like.

The theatre at St Albans—
as it is now

This is what it looked
like in Roman times

Theatre of Marcellus

The only theatre left in Rome is the theatre of Marcellus. It was dedicated by Augustus to his nephew Marcellus, who died in 23 BC. This was the second largest in Rome with 12,000 seats. (The theatre of Pompey, which had 40,000, has not survived.) All that remains of it now is two dozen arches of the outer wall, as you can see in the picture opposite.

In the following passage, Suetonius describes an incident in the theatre:

When Augustus sat down on his chair of state, it gave way and sent him sprawling on his back. A panic started in the audience.... The audience were afraid that the walls might collapse. Augustus, finding he could do nothing to quieten them down, left his own box, and sat among the people, in what seemed to be the most dangerous part of the *auditorium*.

Suetonius *Augustus* 43

Theatre of Marcellus today and (below) a model of it as it used to be

The stage

The picture on the right is a reconstruction of the stage and stage buildings at Sabratha, a Roman colony in North Africa, built in about AD 200. Notice the elaborate roof, the three storeys all of white marble pillars, the statues and doors.

A curtain was used, but it was only three metres high and was fixed in a slot at the front of the stage; it was taken down at the beginning of the play and remained down till the end, when it was raised. The stage even had trap-doors.

Various pieces of stage equipment were used. One could produce the effect of thunder and lightning, another was a crane which hoisted actors up and down (to represent going from earth to heaven and vice versa). Another was a series of revolving screens of painted wood, which represented, for example, the town, the country, the harbour etc.

Reconstruction of Sabratha stage

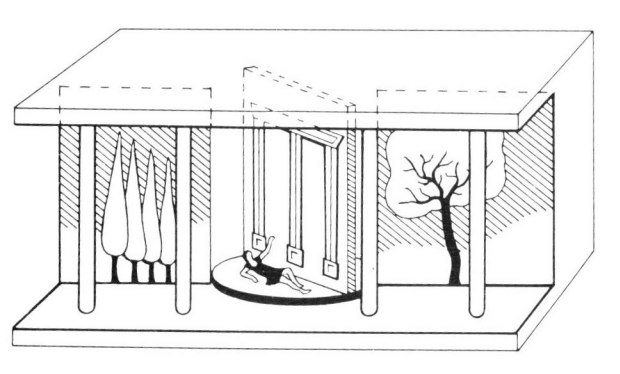

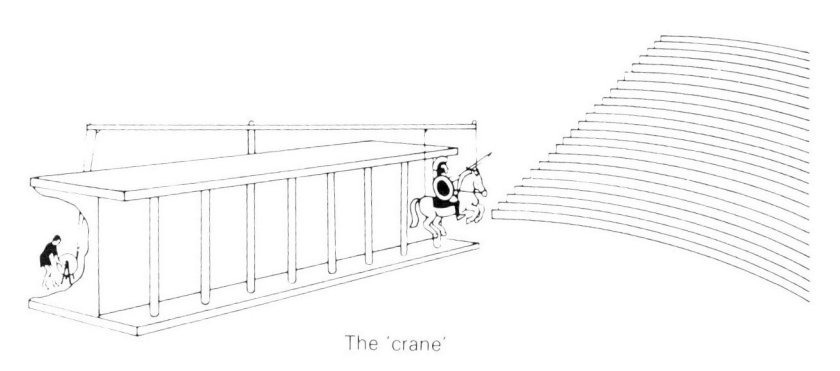

Revolving scenery

The 'crane'

The audience

The audience in a Roman theatre had to sit for long hours on stone seats and under a hot sun. Not surprisingly, the organiser of the show went out of his way to provide comforts for them.

First canvas covers gave protection from the sun (see page 36); many people brought parasols with them as well as cushions to sit on. The stage and seats were often sprinkled with a perfume made from saffron (a plant) to reduce the smell of sweat.

The organiser also provided food, drinks, and sweets at the performance, though spectators often brought their own food with them. On special occasions, the audience received free gifts—for example, in Nero's reign, 1,000 assorted birds daily, food parcels, and vouchers for corn, clothes, gold, silver, pearls, paintings, slaves, animals, ships, houses, and farms!

Roman audiences were difficult to please. Once they were so bored with a performance of Terence's play *Hecyra* that they left the theatre to watch some tight-rope walkers. And—like modern audiences—if they didn't like the play they whistled and hissed. If the performance was bad enough, they threw apples!

Musicians performed during the play. In this mosaic you can see (from left to right) a female flute-player, a man with mini-cymbals, and another with a tambourine

Nero on the stage

The Emperor Nero believed that his voice was divine (actually it was rather feeble) and often performed on the public stage. He hired a group of youths to applaud him wherever he went. They were divided into three sections according to the noise they produced: the Bees made a loud humming sound, the Tiles clapped with their hands cupped, and the Bricks clapped with flat hands.

No one was allowed to leave the theatre during his recitals, even in an emergency, and the doors were kept shut. We hear of women in the audience giving birth, and of men being so bored with the music and applause that they secretly dropped down the back wall, or pretended to be dead and were carried away for burial.

Nero suffered from stage-fright and 'nerves' and was very jealous of his rivals. Though usually gracious and charming in front of the other competitors, he often insulted them behind their backs. And if any were particularly good singers, he would bribe them to sing badly.

Plays

Plays were of two types, tragedies (serious plays) and comedies. The Romans preferred comedies.

As the plays were performed in the open air, Roman producers had two main problems: getting the audience to hear the words and to see who the main characters were. The answer was simple: the actors wore special masks and costumes.

On this page you can see a tragic and a comic mask; these were often so grotesque that they used to terrify young children. The large mouth also acted as a loudspeaker.

Most characters could be recognised as soon as they stepped on to the stage. Old men, for example, usually had long, white beards, and slaves wore red wigs. Other familiar characters included evil slave dealers, foolish young men, and innocent young girls.

The most popular character of all was the slave. Audiences loved to see the slave make a fool of their elderly masters, because such a thing was, of course, unlikely in real life.

A tragic mask

A comic mask

'The Menaechmus Brothers'

One of the funniest Roman playwrights was Plautus, who was writing comedies in about 220 BC. Here is a scene from one of his plays, *The Menaechmus Brothers*:

(This is about two identical twins called Menaechmus, who were separated at birth and grew up in different cities: Menaechmus I in Epidamnus, Menaechmus II in Syracuse. At the beginning of the play Menaechmus II returns to Epidamnus, and the fun starts when he is mistaken for his brother.

In this scene Menaechmus II pretends to be mad to escape from Menaechmus I's wife and father-in-law, who promptly summon a doctor to examine him. Then, of course, Menaechmus I appears.)

Doctor How are you, Menaechmus? Dear me, why have you uncovered your arm? Don't you know that only makes it worse?

Menaechmus Why don't you go and get lost?

Old man What do you think?

Doctor Well, I'm sure drugs won't help. Now, look, Menaechmus!

Menaechmus What do you want?

Doctor Answer my questions, please. Do you take your wine black?

Menaechmus Go to the devil.

Old man That's his madness coming on.

Menaechmus Why not ask whether I eat purple bread or yellow bread, or red bread if it comes to that? Or if I eat birds with scales or fish with feathers?

Old man Oh dear, oh dear, do you hear how he's raving? What are you waiting for? Give him some medicine before he has a fit.

Doctor Just a minute. I have more questions to ask.

Old man This talk will be the death of him.

Doctor Tell me, are your eyes ever swollen?

Menaechmus What do you think I am, you clown, a grasshopper?

Doctor Tell me, does your stomach ever rumble?

Menaechmus When I'm full, no; when I'm empty, yes.

Doctor He doesn't sound like a madman. Do you sleep well at nights?

Menaechmus When I've no debts on my conscience, if it's any of your business.

Doctor Now he's beginning to rave. Watch out when he talks like that.

Old man He's talking better than he was before—he called his wife an old cow!

Menaechmus I said what?

Old man You were mad, I tell you.

Menaechmus Me?

Old man Yes, you! You threatened to run me down with a chariot! I'm telling you, that's what you said. I know!

Menaechmus And I know that you stole Jupiter's sacred wreath; and I know that you were put into prison for it; and I know that you were flogged when they let you out; and I know that you killed your father and sold your mother. There, are you satisfied? Have I insulted you as much as you insulted me?

A scene from a comedy. On the left, two old men. In the middle, a flute-player. On the right, a drunken young man supported by a slave

'The Ghost'

Another of Plautus' comedies was called *The Mostellaria*, or 'The Ghost'. The plot is simple: while his father is away on business, a young man called Philolaches is having a riotous time, spending his father's money on parties and girls and assisted by his slave Tranio. Suddenly the old man returns, while there is a party going on. The slave must prevent the old man going into the house, so he invents a fantastic story.

(*The old man walks up to the front door. The slave watches him from the side.*)

Old man What's this? The door locked, in broad daylight? (*Knocks*) Hello, is anyone in? Open up!

Slave Who's this at our front door?

Old man Why, it's my slave Tranio.

Slave Greetings, master, I'm glad to see you safe and well. You *are* well?

Old man Of course. Anyone can see that. But what about you? Have you gone mad?

Slave Pardon?

Old man There's something wrong. There's no reply at the door. I knocked several times.

Slave (*Horrified*) You touched the door?

Old man Of course I touched it. In fact, I nearly broke it down.

Slave You actually—touched it?

Old man Yes, I touched it, I touched it!

Slave O ye gods!

Old man What's wrong?

Slave Something—terrible!

Old man What do you mean?

Slave You must get away from here, now! Run for your life! You're cursed!

Old man Look, what's this all about? Tell me, for pity's sake!

Slave No one has set foot in the house for seven months.

Old man What on earth for?

Slave (*Pretends to hear something*) Listen! Did you hear that?

Old man (*Looks around nervously*) There's no one here. Now tell me—

Slave A dreadful deed was done—

Old man What was done? I don't understand.

Slave The man who sold you the house murdered one of his guests.

Old man Murdered him?

Slave Then he robbed him and buried him in the garden.

Old man Good heavens!

Slave One night, we all went to bed—we were all asleep, when suddenly it came—

Old man What do you mean, 'it'?

Slave The ghost, of course. Your son saw it and heard it.

Old man Heard it?

Slave It said, 'My name is Diapontius. I am a stranger from overseas and was once a guest in this house. I was cruelly murdered in my sleep and robbed. Now I cannot enter the Underworld, because I didn't receive a proper burial. No one can live here happily now. You must all leave. This place has my curse.'

Since then, master, there have been terrible goings-on here.

Old man   Sh! Listen!
Slave   Heavens, what was that?
Old man   The door rattled!
Slave   Do you think it was—
Old man   I think I'm going to faint!
Slave   (*Aside*) Those fools! They'll ruin my story!
Old man   What did you say?
Slave   Keep away from that door! Run for your life!
Old man   You come with me!
Slave   I've no quarrel with the dead!
Voice inside   Hello-o-o, Tranio!
Slave   No, not me, I didn't knock on the door!
Old man   Who are you talking to?
Slave   Was that you that called me just now? I swear, I thought it was the ghost seeking vengeance. You'd better run as fast as your legs can carry you, and pray to Hercules.
Old man   Hercules, I pray you, help me! (Runs off)
Slave   (*Relieved*) Help me too, Hercules. Give him all he deserves—and more.

An actor going over his lines.
Notice his mask on the right

QUESTIONS

1. What were the shape and appearance of a Greek theatre? (page 49)
2. What were a the *orchestra* (page 49)
       b the *auditorium*? (page 50)
3. What improvements did the Romans make in the theatre? (page 50)
4. What are acoustics? (page 50)
5. What different entertainments were held in St Albans theatre? (page 51)
6. What happened to Augustus during the performance of the play at the theatre of Marcellus? (page 52)
7. What was different about a Roman curtain? (page 53)
8. What special effects could the Romans produce on the stage? (page 53)
9. What comforts were provided for a Roman audience? (page 54)
10. Who were the Bees, Tiles and Bricks? (page 55)
11. Why did the Roman actors wear grotesque masks? (page 56)

THINGS TO DO

1. What is an orchestra today? How do you think the meaning of the word changed? Write down your answers.
2. Draw EITHER a Roman theatre (make sure you label the various parts),
   OR a scene from one of the Roman comedies given here.
3. Make a model of a comic mask. Some help from the Art Department may be needed.
4. What comforts are provided for a modern theatre or cinema audience? Compare them with the kinds of facilities Roman theatres had.
5. Did you find the two extracts on pages 57–60 funny or not? Would they be more or less funny on the stage? Why do you think this is so?
   Act one or both of the extracts and see if you can make your class laugh.

SOME IMPORTANT DATES

	Dates	Events	Writers
BC	753	Foundation of Rome	
	c 500	Circus Maximus built	
	c 400	Great Period of Greek Drama	
	c 200	Plautus' 'Mostellaria' produced	Plautus
	73–71	Revolt of Spartacus	
	55	First stone theatre built	Cicero
	27–	Reign of Augustus	
AD	14	Theatre of Marcellus built (**11 BC**)	Ovid
	37–41	Reign of Caligula	
	41–54	Reign of Claudius	
		Improvements made to Circus	
	54–68	Reign of Nero	Seneca
		Riot at Pompeii (**59**)	
	69	Reign of Vitellius	
	69–79	Reign of Vespasian	
		Colosseum started	
	79–81	Reign of Titus	
		Colosseum finished, Eruption of Vesuvius	
	81–96	Reign of Domitian	Martial
	98–117	Reign of Trajan	Pliny, Tacitus
	117–138	Reign of Hadrian	Suetonius, Juvenal
	404	Abolition of Gladiator shows by Emperor Honorius	